The Stones Speak

Poetry by Fay Picardi
Art by Cindy Michaud

Copyright 2011 Burnt Umber Press

ISBN-13: 978-1463569082

ISBN-10: 1463569084

BURNT UMBER PRESS

CONTENTS

Preface

The Stones Speak. 1

The Past Laid Bare 7

The Connections Built. 19

The Relevance Revealed 33

The Stones Speak Still. 45

We dedicate this book lovingly to
Kathy Garvey,
our friend, our muse and our editor.
Without her it would not exist.

PREFACE

If you have ever held a stone in the palm of your hand and been fascinated by its form, its composition, or its past, this exploration is for you.

Stones have been around for more than 3 billion years. Stone tools have been discovered and dated at 1.8 million years. Man has used stone for shelter, roadways, borders and bridges. Contained within stones are accurate records of weather cycles, temperature changes and upheavals in the earth's crust. In modern times stones have provided data for history and metaphor for expression. A small stone held in your hand today may have first been found in the Baltic Sea or held by an ancient Ethiopian.

For those who admire stone, there is no end to the inspiration it provides. As the two of us discussed our mutual fascination, we had very little hesitation that "stone" could become the focus of a creative, collaborative effort. And while the subject held a mutual (and we hoped universal) appeal, we also recognized that neither of us would share the same experiences nor use the same lens in examining how best to offer our impressions.

Thus, as we put our senses, our pasts and our imaginations to work, we sought to illustrate, in poetry or art, what the stones said to us individually. In some cases, our paths crossed. In others, they did not. Our hope is that you may have already heard some of these same messages. Or that our work will inspire you to pick up a stone and listen to it speak in a new way.

Cindy Michaud and Fay Picardi

THE STONES SPEAK

THE STONES SPEAK

24" x 18"
Acrylic and Graphite

THE STONES SPEAK

I
More than three billion years, they say,
before we were born,
the stones were.
They moved from place to place
like nomads
leaving their remains
strewn across the continents.
They will never finish their journeys,
but wherever they are,
they give evidence to their travels;
they tell the story of the age
when they were moving the earth
and changing all that was in it,
including themselves.

II
With many voices, the stones speak.
They are waiting for us to listen.
We are here, they say.
You will see us along the roadsides.
You will hear us in the rush of wave.
You will smell us as you run over the moss.
You will taste us in your bread.
You will feel us in the warmth that sustains you.
We support your nourishing ground.
We wait under your prayers.
How can you live without us?
All history is here.
All substance is contained within each one of us.
Listen. Listen.

III
And what can we know of the future?
First, we must understand the past;
we must trust the present;
we must use our eyes to see,
our hands to hold one simple stone
and know to listen when it speaks.

THE PAST LAID BARE

SISYPHEAN, INDEED

24" x 18"
Acrylic and Graphite

FROM THE ATHENS SUBWAY

What fascinates me
are the strata,
layer on layer of stones
of rubble
of refuge.
The debris of any civilization
defines it.

Athens was built on Athens,
was built on Athens,
was built on Athens,
is built on Athens.
One millennium on top of the next
until today the taxi drivers
run over the worn stone roadways
without a thought of what has come before.

In the Athens Metro
where progress preserves the past,
anyone who wants to
can stand and see the past laid bare.
Surer than any history,
it is revealed bit by bit.
A broken vessel here,
a coffin there,
some bones, some stones.
Strata after strata, telling man's story
with what remains of joys and griefs.

THE STONES LAID BARE

6" x 8"
Stone Assemblage

FOSSIL SQUID

Somewhere in the Moroccan desert,
an ancient lake has been uncovered,
reclaimed from the sands.

3 billion years or more ago,
its waters held the beginnings of life.
3 billion years ago,
it nurtured all that was to come.

Now, I hold in my hand one small stone,
hardened and polished by time,
an incarnation of the past,
in concentric circles of grey and black.
It is a gift given by the universe
whose whys and wherefores
we continue to seek.

FROM THE PETROGLYPHS

Ancestral Puebloans
pounded their wonder
into volcanic rock

With small stones,
they chiseled their faiths
into desert varnish.

From the beginning of time
their message stands still.
Believe. Believe.

THE GRAVESTONES AT PISA

In the Camposanto Cloister,
where noble Pisans are buried in sacred soil
brought back by Crusaders from Golgotha,
the gravestones have carved angels
even children can draw,
and dream about at night.

In daylight, each child creates his own disaster,
imagines his own death so many times over
that when death comes and is not a game,
without thinking, he asks that familiar figure in.

I've known only singular deaths.
Each coming, one by one,
and devastating my life,
once and then again.
Dress in orange or black, it doesn't matter.
Each one takes a hand, a shoulder—my heart,
some part of me and attaches itself.

Not one of them will stay asleep;
each insists on visiting in the night
or whispering in my ear at twilight.
I do not want them under carved stones,
these deaths, but they have brokered stones,
and must claim their immortality.

STONES ON STONE

In the Cemetery Montparnasse,
three small stones atop one burial slab
and each one painted as if by a child.
One red, one blue, one with a touch of pink.

I am too old to be learning
of this custom for the first time,
this leaving of stones on graves.
But I can imagine why they were left.
I can supply six million stories
of who and what and when.

I would have a story of my own;
I would make this grave, my grave.
I would make these stones, my stones.
I would let these three stones tell the world;
some of those whom I loved
are still among the living.

STONE SERENADE

24" x 18"
Acrylic and Graphite

THE CONNECTIONS BUILT

CROSSING INTO SAFETY

24" x 18"
Acrylic and Graphite

SILENT SENTINEL

24" x 18"
Acrylic and Graphite

DRY WALLING STONE

At Paestum
ancient Greeks built their temples.
Stone on stone the columns rise
telling stories of the years
when the sea ran along the edge of the town.

In those days, no one used mortar.
The masons fitted stone on stone
as naturally as we can fit
the arch of one foot
into the other.

Today, poppies dot the old stone pathways of Paestum.
Buttercups peek from behind foundation rocks.
Three temples still stand silhouetted against the sky.

In our world, there are too few men
who can dry wall stone;
who can pile one stone carefully upon another
until the whole is so much greater than its parts.
In our world, we are almost always in need of mortar.

HEARTING

18" x 18"
Acrylic and Graphite

CAIRN

We never quite know when friendship begins
or exactly why. One day, it's just there,
plain as can be, waiting to be embraced.

Perhaps it comes when someone helps
without being asked. Or when two or three of us
share an unexpected laugh.
Maybe it begins with some special gift,
handmade and one of a kind.

Some believe cairns are a symbol of friendship,
a solid memorial, a symbol of respect.

Somewhere in the Blue Ridge Mountains,
somewhere right in the middle of the New River
which flows from the home of my ancestors,
my friends have built a cairn for me.

I can go there in my mind,
can find calm with just a thought,
can watch the sun and water change the colors,
change the form of each stone.

Although I do not want to lose them,
I know someday these stones, too,
will be swept into the flow of the universe,
will disappear into the river
only to reappear who knows when or where.

What will not disappear is their beauty
or the friendship they represent.

EVIDENCE OF TRAVEL

20" x 12"
Acrylic and Graphite

STANDING ON THE PRECIPICE

(A Visit to the Irish Hunger Memorial, NYC)

The stone is jagged
at the tip of Achill Island,
the promontory sticking out
like the bow of a ship,
and the wind whistling round
no matter the day.

Looking West from there,
I once tried to conjure
the image of grandfathers so far back
the greats cannot be reckoned.
We all have those memories,
Irish or no.
We see the John Kennedy Ireland,
admire the thatched huts,
think of the potato famine,
applaud the red headed beauty
setting out at sixteen to find
her fortune in the New World.

Now I stand on another promontory
in the midst of New York City,
looking over the sound
at Ellis Island.
I have walked the long tunnel
leading to the hill;
listened to the haunting of dirges.
I have climbed the rugged pathway,
passed stones carved with the names
of places that are etched in my bones.
County Mayo, County Galway, County Claire.
The memories of thousands
float up to me through the fall air;
those who have died of hunger;
those who have survived.

ON THE EDGE

12" x 12"
Acrylic and Graphite

SEASONS

24" x 27"
Acrylic and Graphite

THE RELEVANCE REVEALED

DRANESVILLE PARK

I
Her creator called her Penelope,
but that was only because
her husband had not come home.

What she really meant
was that she hated the waiting,
and who wouldn't
alone so far from town
and surrounded by wilderness.

She tended the children and the garden.
In dry weather, she filled the cistern with water
from the spring that ran to the river
down the mountain from her log cabin.
She gathered twigs and branches for the fire
and not even the fog could cover her loneliness.

II
But none of this happened.
There was only a tall chimney
and a hearth waiting for its next fire.
There were steps, bits and pieces of foundation,
a cistern waiting for the next fill.
All of stone. All crumbling.

III
Making stories is what we do,
for ourselves or others,
whether we realize it or not.
Creating lives is what peoples us.
If only we could control the plot.

ALL THAT REMAINS

18" x 14"
Acrylic and Graphite

HEAL, HEAL

It's spring that brings new life,
a surge of green, a hint of Frost's gold.
In the dead of winter,
it's the survival of the fittest.

My only cousin and I stand at the edge
of Dunlap Creek, remembering
our childhood summers.
Now, the life we see
is the slow moving art of winter.
Trout swimming in dark circles
deep beneath the old diving board.
The freezing water making eddies
in and around the ice.
Creek stones being rounded
by the clear, cold flow.

My cousin strips off his coat,
his flannel shirt and shoes,
then dives into the frigid water,
swims a few strokes,
and comes up shaking
the creek water off his skin
as a dog would shake his fur.
He climbs the bank,
puts on his clothes
and strikes out for the car.

Usually, this man is a man of many words.
He has charmed and seduced.
Almost sixty, with eight children
by nearly as many women,
he seems some type of tent show healer,
shouting his message to the world.

He has come here to perform an exorcism
without incantations. He has immersed himself
in the only holy water he has ever known,
has been praying, silently, to another healer,
hoping to cast out the raging cancer.

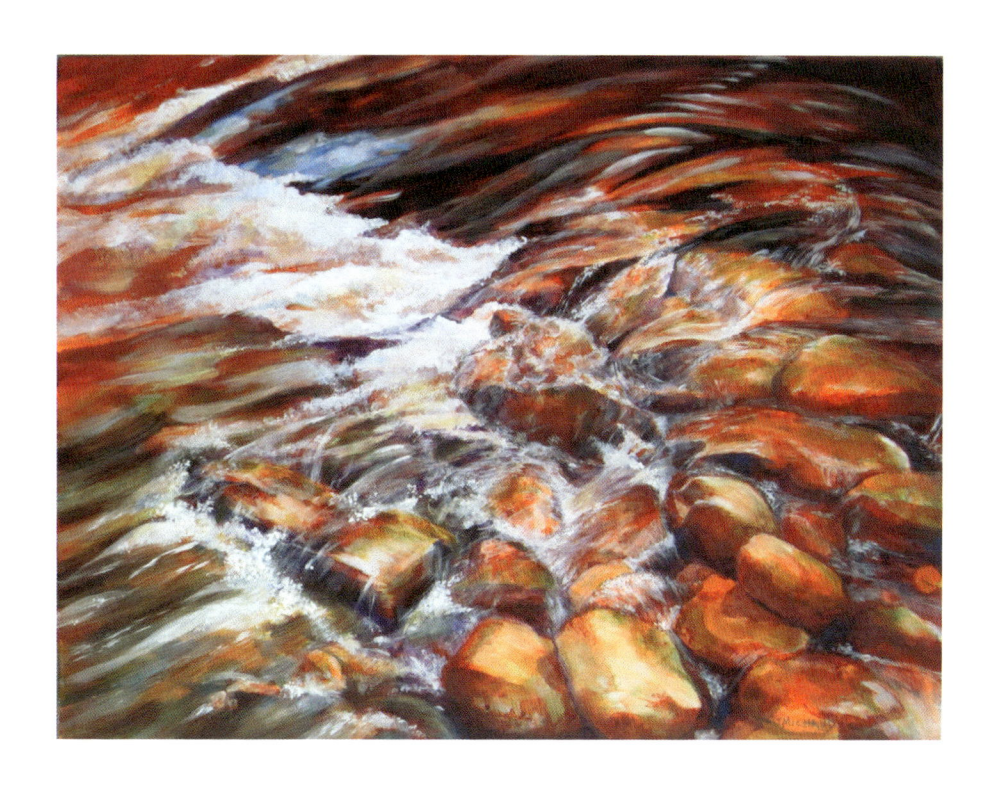

STONES OF THE RIVER

18" x 24"
Acrylic and Graphite

ROCA ROJA

18" x 24"
Acrylic and Graphite

THE HOPI WAY

When a Hopi child strays
from time honored ways,
a member of the tribe takes his hand,
gently repeats the words of the elders.
"That is not the Hopi way."

Tradition is the Hopi way.
3rd Mesa. Stone pit bread.
Kachina dolls. Ceremonial dances.
Talismani. Fetishes.

Hopi child, gather your stones.
Gather stones that resemble mountains.
Tukwi. Tukwi.

Try to remember.
Power is not what you hold in your hand.
Power is what you believe.

STONE SOUP
10" x 20"
Mixed Media

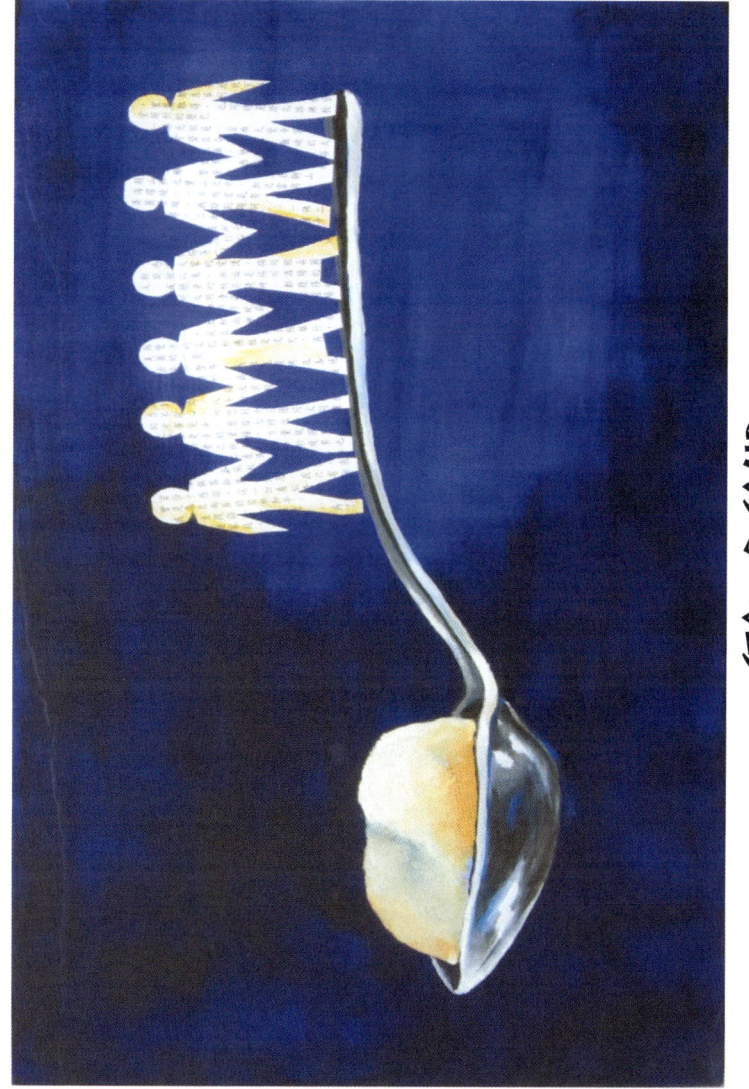

SKIPPING STONES

I watched my uncle skip
    a stone across the creek,
clear creek and cold.
(It made a path of magic circles
    which widened as we watched.

I stood in wonder
    being only five
at how one tiny stone
    could create a way so wide
across the water, I could almost walk.

The circles grew and grew,
    I asked my uncle if
they ever stopped
and he said, no, once
    started they could only grow
and grow.

My uncle was the captain of a ship,
    you know.
He helped to lay the cable
    cross the seas
and brought such treasure as he found
    of boomerangs and grass skirts
back to me.

My uncle knew about such things,
    the way across the water
and how to choose a stone
    and make it skip
in such a way the movement that it started,
    never stopped.

THE STONES SPEAK STILL

STONES SPEAK STILL

24" x 24"
Mixed Media

OLD STONES SONNET

Old stones, my husband calls them.
Roman ruins, pagan altars,
Pompeian foundations,
random relics
of what has past before,
they are all the same to him.

Give him a fishing rod in his hand,
and a boat to take him
into the wilderness.
There, he stalks the pre-historic;

Settles in with no other intent
than to retrace the past
on the remains of the conquered;
One scale at a time.

A CHERRY WHEN IT'S BLOOMIN'

*I gave my love a cherry
That had no stone…
(Old Appalachian Lullaby)*

Cherry blossoms are soft and pink.
They enchant us with their fragile beauty.

In the Loire valley of France,
the cherries farmers grow are so delicious
they haunt the memory for half a century.
They warm the mouth in mid-day,
give birth to sensuous dreams.

Cherry stones are small and hard,
brilliant red and yellow, unmistakable.
Their glossy perfection cleverly belies
the secrets they hide inside.

GREEN STONE PATIO

My father was a working man,
not by occupation, though that too,
but by compulsion.
He moved walls,
added rooms,
built garages, stairways,
churches.

But, at some point,
he fell in love
with green stone from Virginia.
Then he built chimneys,
covered hearths and mantels,
and once, when I came home,
he had constructed
in the back yard among the dogwood,
a flagstone patio
large enough for forty.

What is it about stone?
An old foundation,
a still standing chimney,
a simple stone to kick in the road.

Michelangelo must have known.
His *Slaves* immerge right out of the marble.
He said the stone spoke to him.
Most sculptors do.

My dad was not a sculptor,
not a stone mason, not an artist.
Yet, he knew
the stone would talk to him.
As to the caveman,
to the farmer,
to us all.

If we listen, we can hear so much;
What we know of ourselves
and of the world.

WHO'S JIVIN' WHO?

Saturday night blues
echoing round black town
Vicksburg, Miss. 1955.
Polestar shakin' to a sax,
sound pourin' over crushed stones,
hotter than the core of the earth
and louder. Volcano eruptions.

3 billion years ago,
(or was it 3.5?)
the earth started movin'
to its own music.
5 billion more, they say,
and the fire will be gone,
the dancin' done.

Does this surprise me?
I know what I know.
Life comes.
Life goes away.
The music stops.
The stones stay.

STORIES REMEMBERED

12" x 12"
Mixed Media

PREVIOUS LIFETIMES

12" x 12"
Mixed Media

ANCIENT PASSAGES

12" x 12"
Mixed Media

PLACES TRAVELLED

12" x 12"
Mixed Media

ARTIST'S END NOTES

The Stones Speak
Sometimes a stone speaks of its own story, at other times it speaks on behalf of the man who alters it. This painting is a collection of significant and recognizable stones manipulated by man in an effort to leave a message for future generations.

Bare Stones
The small, black stone begged for a fossil to be drawn upon it but the others were simply arranged. This assemblage reminds me that nature is always the master artisan.

Sisyphean, Indeed
The story of Sisyphus and his condemnation to forever push a stone up a steep incline caused me to question the most impossible task humans face today. The headlines were of the tsunami in Japan as well as other natural disasters around the globe. I knew that no matter what we do to "save the earth" it really is a futile task; Mother Nature will have her way, major changes have gone before us and more are ahead: we are a very tiny speck on the time line.

Stone Serenade
These stones along a favorite hiking trail have often provided a background serenade for serious contemplation.

Crossing into Safety
This is taken from a stream off the Blue Ridge Parkway where I have watched many tackle the crossing, some with confidence and others with great fear. These stones represent the difficulty we face getting to a "safe place." The title was inspired by one of my favorite Wallace Stenger novels.

Silent Sentinel
As people canoe down this river, or take the drive along River Road, few stop to think about those who preceded them centuries ago. This stone wall stands as a majestic guardian observing it all, yet revealing nothing.

Hearting
The title is a dry walling term which refers to the small, sharply shaped stones used to hold the larger pieces in place. The quotations I painted go to the "heart of the matter," asking all the questions I, too, ask when it comes to building walls in our lives.

Evidence of Travel
While cairns have traditionally been used to mark trail ways and paths,

in some cultures they are used in worship, in marking graves and as calendars. It also occurred to me that the lines, marks, shapes and materials of each of these stones reveal the path of the stone's travel as well.

On the Edge
I can only imagine how this stone must feel looking at a world that seemingly has no place or respect for it in its present form.

Seasons
Stones connect us, literally and figuratively, in many ways. In using a bridge for this message, I wanted to leave those specific connections to the viewer. We do not usually attribute hearts or souls to stone, but we must remember that they, like us, not only survive but are affected by the seasons of time.

All That Remains
An abandoned chimney in Foscoe, NC has captured my imagination for years. Its stones have outlasted the family that gathered them and made them part of their household. The memories and the stones are all that is left. The painting is from this chimney as well as one I photographed while biking in Todd, NC.

Stones of the River
Watching water flow over stones is as hypnotic and soothing as watching flames dance in a fire.

Roca Roja
The red rocks of Sedona provoke awe. They are a vortex of energy for some and the final undoing of others. They hide surprises.

Stone Soup
I loved this story as a child and believed that it taught sharing. Imagine my surprise when the librarian commented that I was checking out "a children's book on collectivism." So is it?

Stones Speak Still
For fun I asked: what do the stones speak about? Could I take this question and portray the answer literally? I had four answers and made a quartet of "stand alones" that easily could hang as one. The answers follow top, left to right, then bottom: They speak of *"Stories Remembered"* illustrated by pieces torn from magazines articles; they speak of *"Previous Lifetimes"* illustrated by materials that were previously used as sandpaper, tea bags, shopping bags and thread; they speak of *"Ancient Passages"* illustrated by using old pieces of toweling and filters; and they speak of *"Places Travelled"* illustrated by strata-like layers made from maps and words of signage along the way.

POET'S END NOTES

From the Athens Subway
When the people of Athens protested the building of the subway in central Athens because they didn't want the remains of their civilization to be disturbed, the city decided to make the central subway stations into modern archeological museums by preserving and revealing the layers of years through Plexiglas plates several stories high and by housing mini museums in upper levels of the entrances.

Fossil Squid
The inspiration for this poem comes from a fossil stone on a necklace which I bought for a friend. The fossil came from a dig site in the Moroccan desert on what was once a lake. It is purported to be more than 3 billion years old.

The Gravestones at Pisa
The Camposanto Cloister is part of Piazza dei Miracoli in Pisa, which includes the Cathedral, the Leaning Tower, and the Baptistery. In addition to the sculptures, sepulchers, and frescoes found in the cloister, the floor is covered with burial stones from the 12th century to the Renaissance.

Dry Walling Stone
Paestum is the site of an ancient Greek and Roman city west of Salerno, Italy. The three temples there are more intact than the Parthenon and one can see the streets and foundations of the houses laid out clearly in the fields of flowers.

Standing on the Precipice
The Irish Hunger Memorial is found at the tip of Manhattan, looking over the bay toward Ellis Island. It honors those who died during the Potato Famine, both in Ireland and while trying to emigrate. It contains stones from every county in Ireland and a stone cottage from County Mayo, the same county in which Achill Island is located.

Dranesville Park
Dranesville Park is located on Georgetown Pike in Virginia along the Potomac River. The Pike and the land around it was surveyed by George Washington.

The reference to the Penelope legend is from a poem about Dranesville Park that I wrote earlier.

Heal, Heal

This poem references Robert Frost's poem, *Nothing Gold Can Stay,* which begins, "Nature's first green is gold, it's hardest hue to hold."

Dunlap Creek is located in Alleghany County, Virginia, and was once the site of a public swimming hole and picnic area developed by my grandfather in the 1930s.

The Hopi Way

Tukwi refers to a stone resembling a mountain which was sometimes used by the Hopi Indians on religious altars or in corn bins as a petition to the gods for a better corn crop.

ABOUT FAY PICARDI

An internationally published poet, Fay Picardi has twice been selected as an artist-in-residence at the Atlantic Center for the Arts as well as a Summer Fellow in Poetry at the University of Virginia. She has worked and studied with two United States Poet Laureates—Anthony Hecht and William Stafford. Recently, she was one of the creators, participants, and editors of *Transformations*, a collaborative art-poetry project and book sponsored by the Brevard Art Museum and the Florida Institute of Technology.

Fay considers herself a daughter of Appalachia and her experiences there have inspired much of her poetry. She has published one book, *Kentucky Poems*, and a chapbook, *Nana's Sunday Dance*, in addition to several limited edition chapbooks such as *From the Petroglyphs*. Her poems have appeared in *Potomac Review*, *Kalliope*, and *Jabberwock*, and other literary works and magazines such as *The Journal of Kentucky Studies* and *Krax*, a British humor magazine. Currently, she is working on two new chapbooks and a novel about Simonetta Vespucci.

A confirmed Francophile because of the year she spent as a Fulbright scholar teaching and living in a French lycée, Fay continues to travel to France to enjoy its beauty and to renew her knowledge of the language. She also dabbles in interior design, art collecting, and spoiling grandchildren. Except for one month in Italy each year and numerous trips to New York, Washington, and Philadelphia to visit family, friends, and as many art museums as possible, Fay lives in Florida with her husband.

ABOUT CINDY MICHAUD

Cindy Michaud has been a visual artist since 2003 when she returned to the easel after a 30 year hiatus. As a life-long communicator with careers in writing and public relations, she continues to share her stories today via paint.

Her work has been exhibited by the Southeastern Pastel Society, the Fredericksburg (MD) Center for the Arts, the Daytona Beach Art League, the Strawbridge Art League, the Art and Antiques Studio, the Brevard (FL) Arts Council and the Avery County (NC) Arts Council.

In 2008, she challenged herself to illustrate 12 life-statements using figurative studies in oil. After writing stories for each piece she solicited contributions from other women and, in 2009, published the book *She Knew, Finally*, now available on amazon.com.

Intrigued by the challenge of collaboration, she and Fay Picardi, along with editor Kathy Garvey and fellow artist Denette Schweikert, helped conceive and co-chair a yearlong project which paired poets with artists. In 2010 *Transformations* opened to a standing-room-only crowd at the Brevard Museum of Art and became a book of the same name. The joy of working with someone in another media laid the seeds for *The Stones Speak*.

Cindy divides her time between Melbourne Village, Florida and Seven Devils, North Carolina where she finds constant inspiration for her landscapes. She is an avid reader and tennis player and enjoys hiking and kayaking.

JUST A SUIT?

To order copies of this book please visit:
https://www.createspace.com/3626744

To arrange for an exhibit of the poetry and art,
please contact either Fay Picardi or Cindy Michaud.

To contact the poet, Fay Picardi, write to her at faypic@earthlink.net.

To contact the artist, Cindy Michaud, write to her at
art@cindymichaud.com.
You may see more of her work at her website:
http://www.cindymichaud.com or enjoy her art with commentary at
http://cindymichaudart.blogspot.com.

This book was created in InDesign by Kathy Garvey,
Graphic Designer/Editor for Burnt Umber Press.
Fonts: Titles are Matisse, poetry and text are Calisto MT.
Bio photos provided by Debby Hamilton Photography.

BURNT UMBER PRESS